D1737924

ACTIVITY GATO ©

YOU CAN CONTACT US
activitygato@gmail.com

YOU CAN FIND OUR OTHER BOOKS (MORE THAN 50 OTHER BOOKS) ON AMAZON

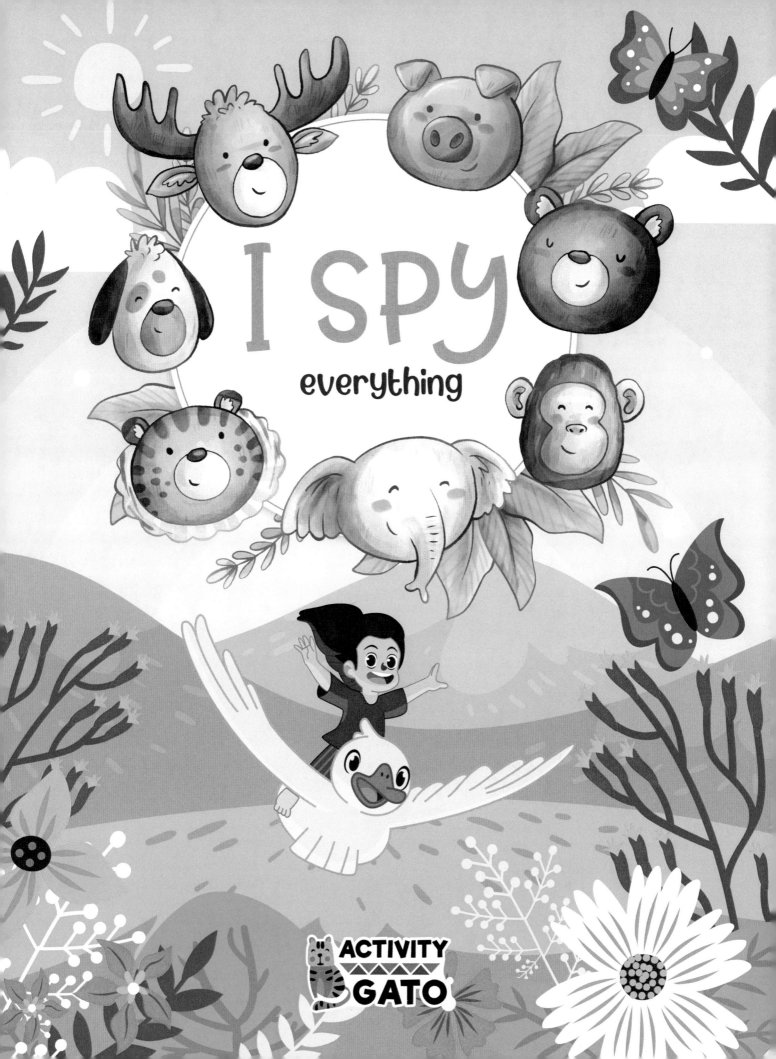

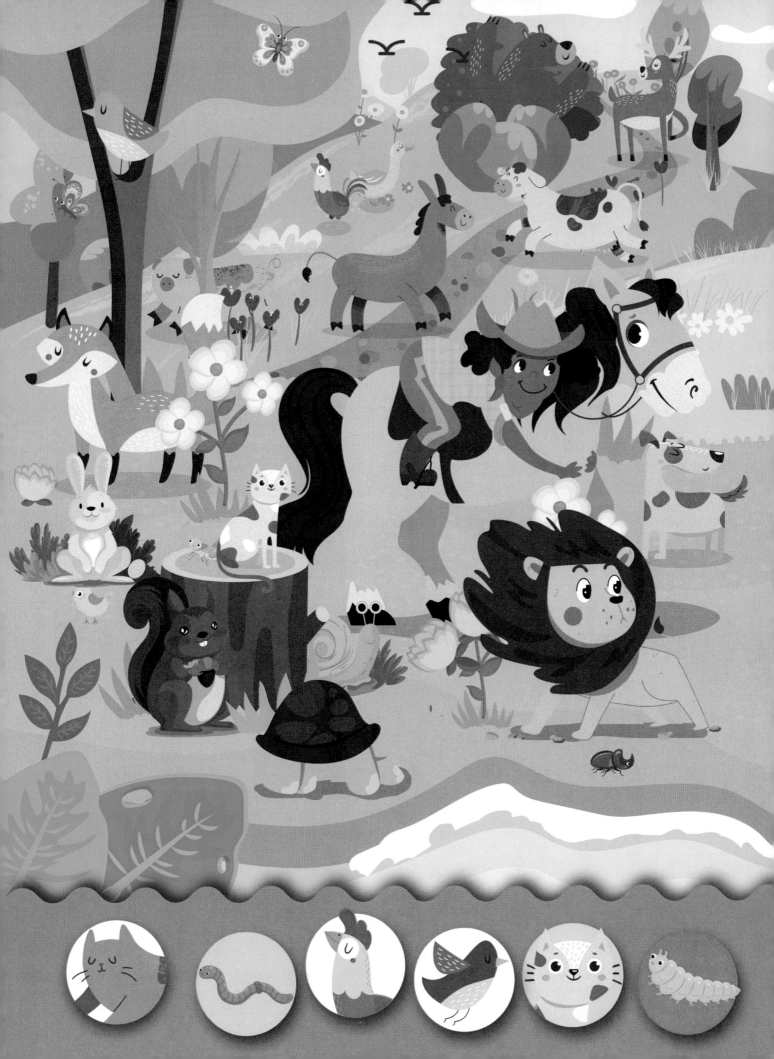

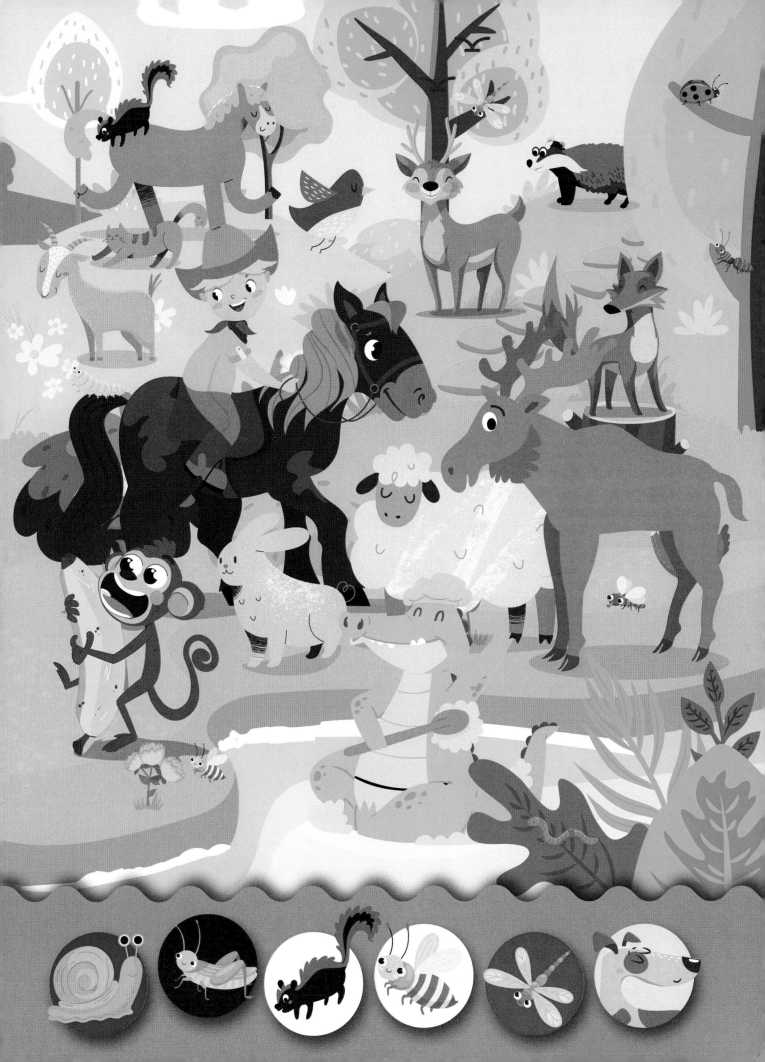

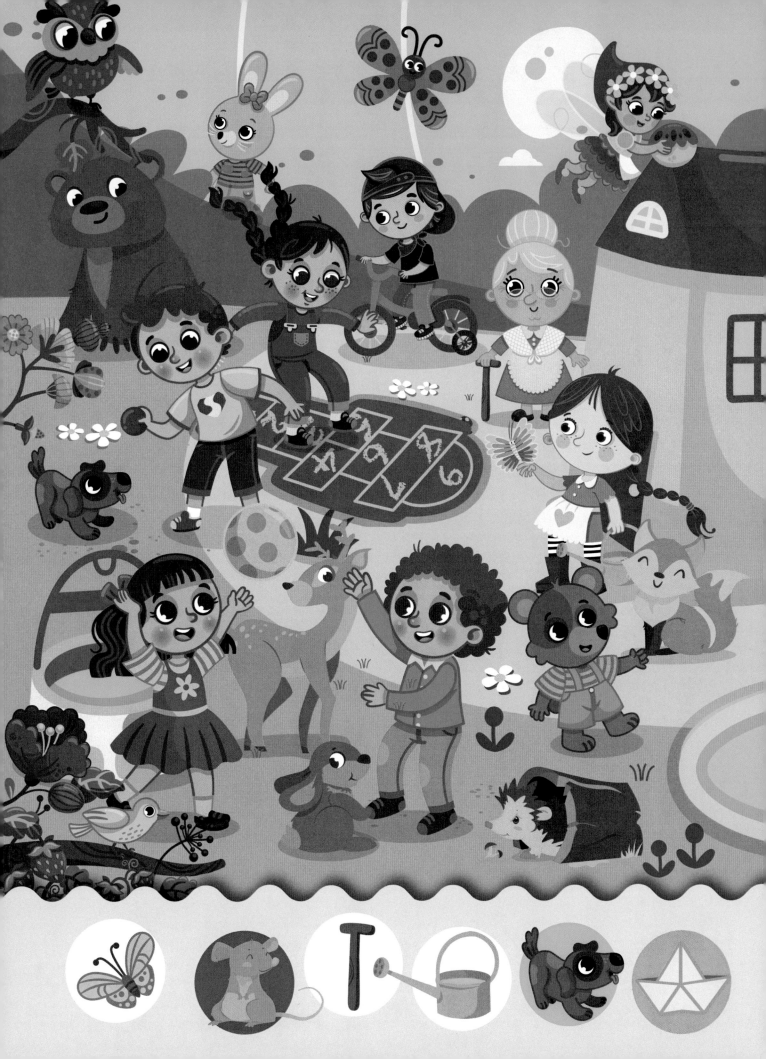

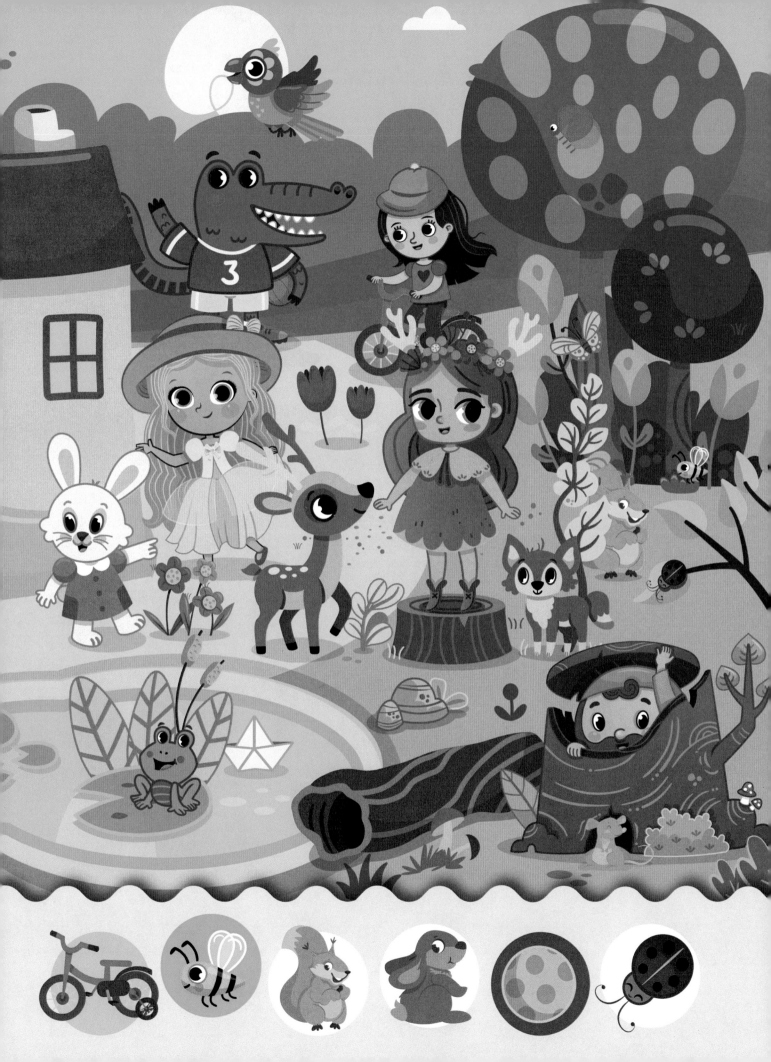

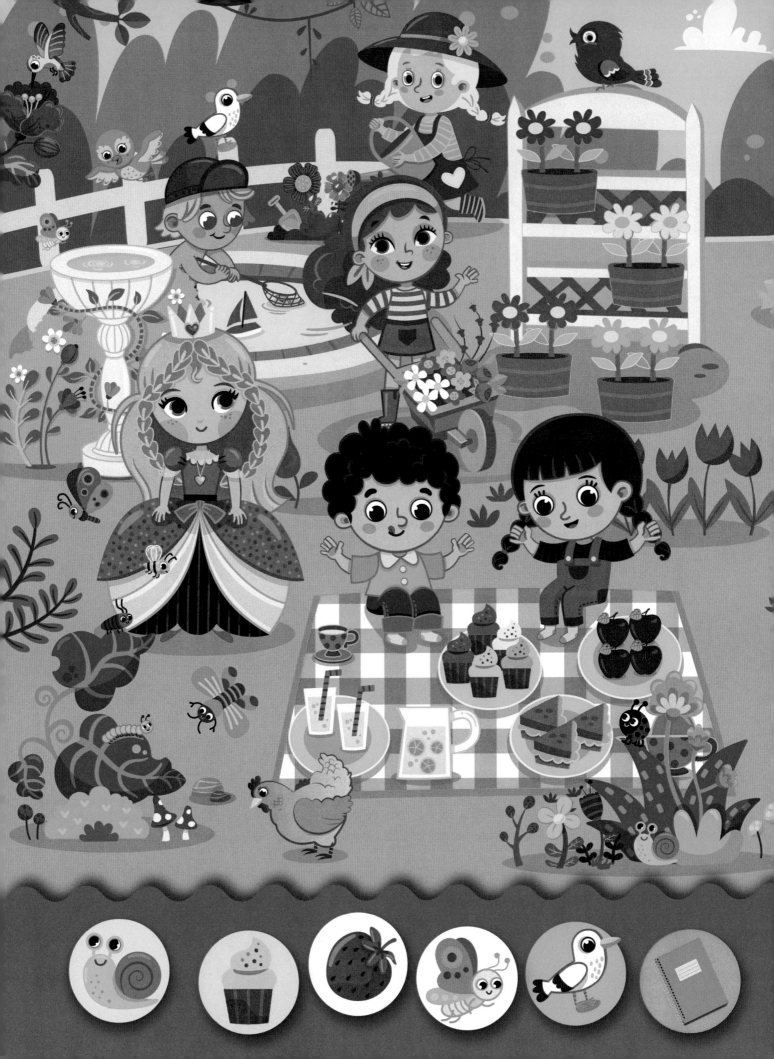

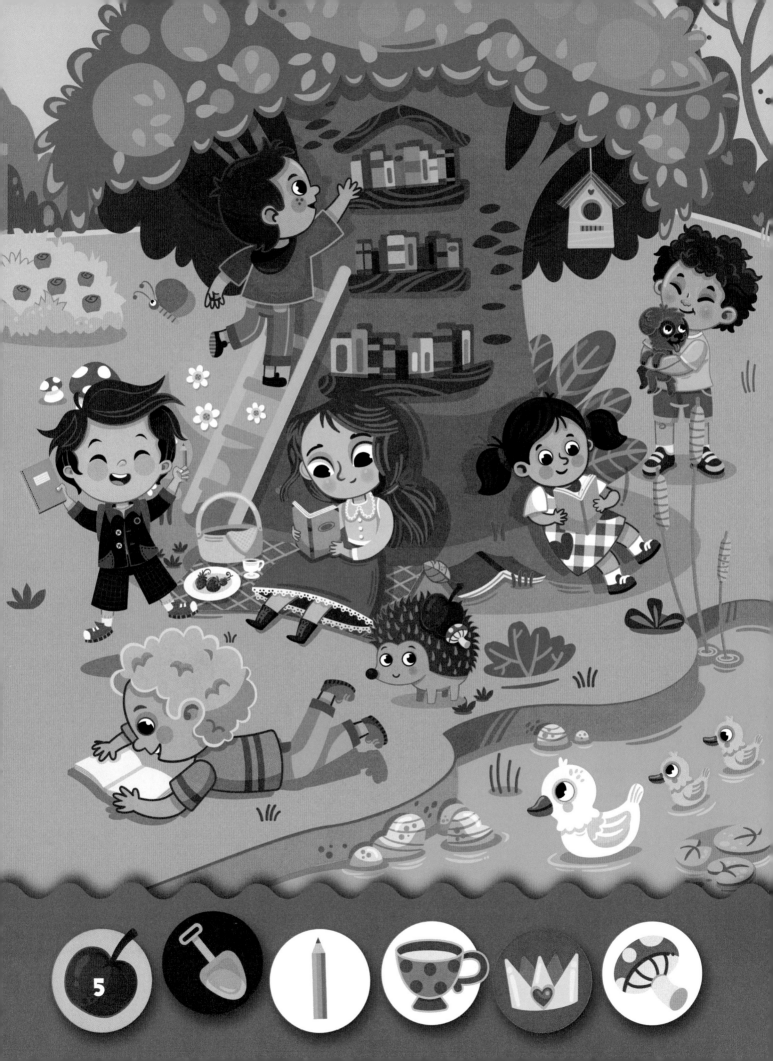

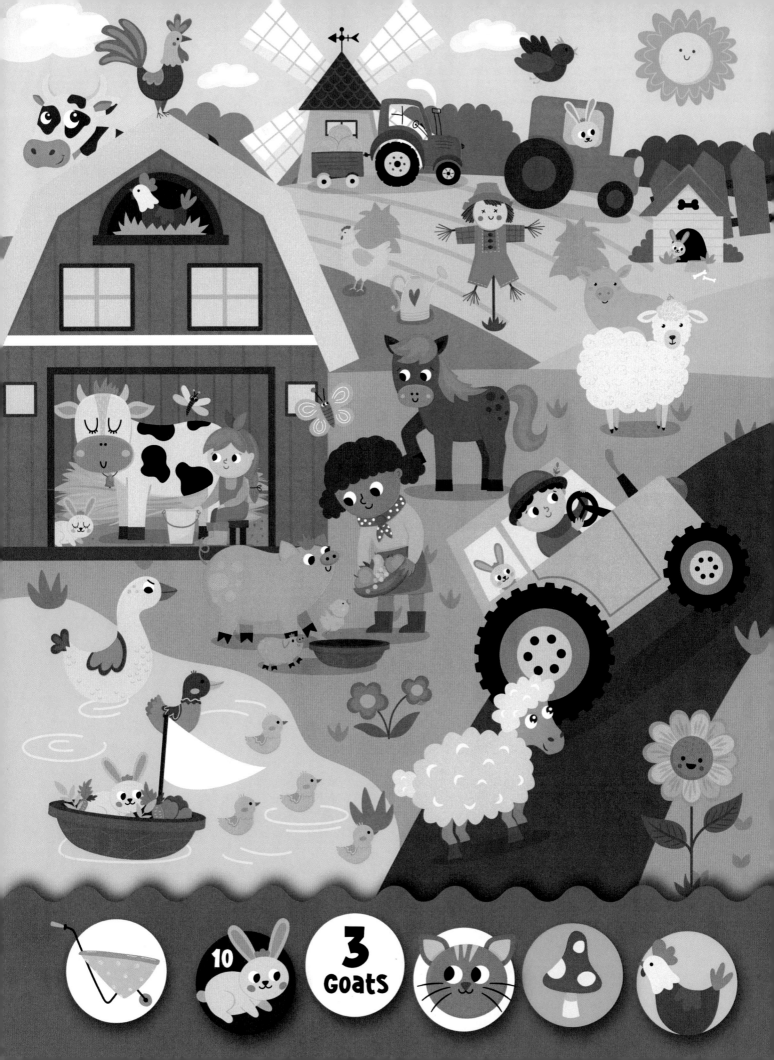

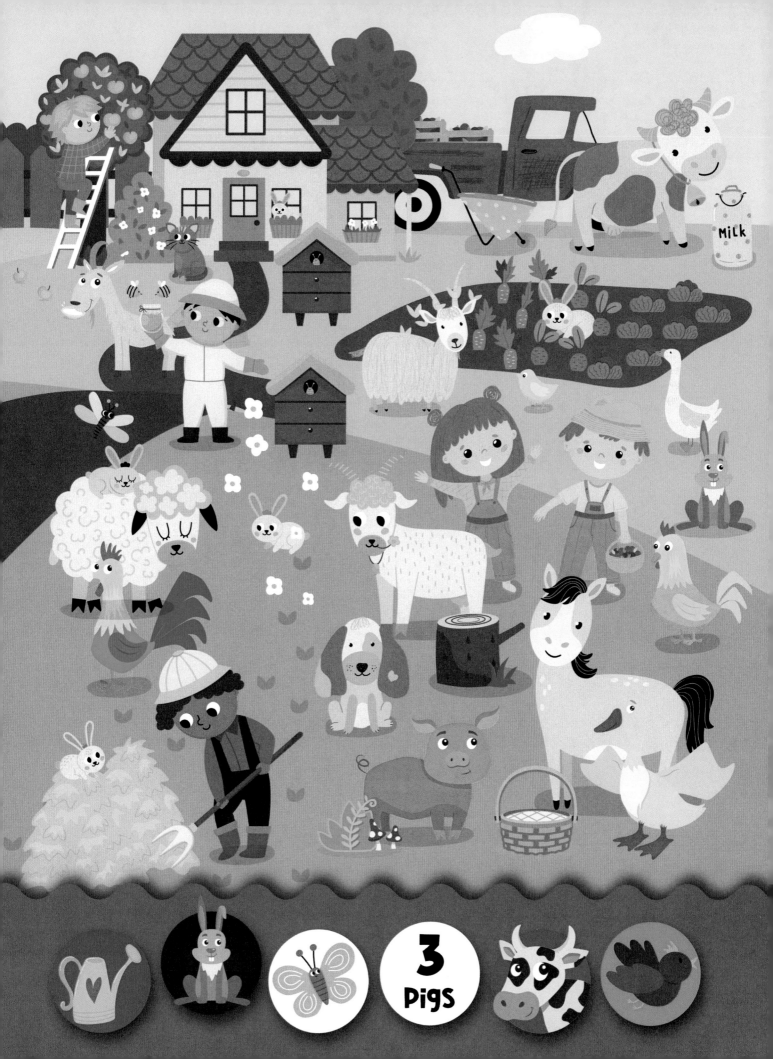

3 Pigs

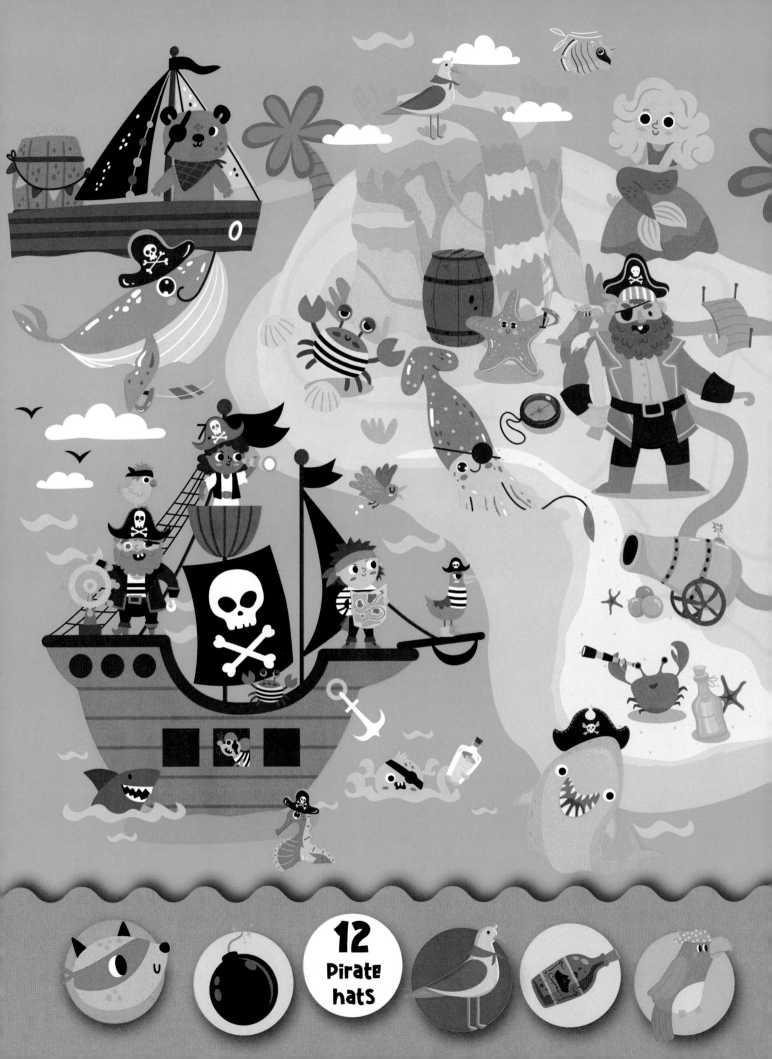

12 Pirate hats

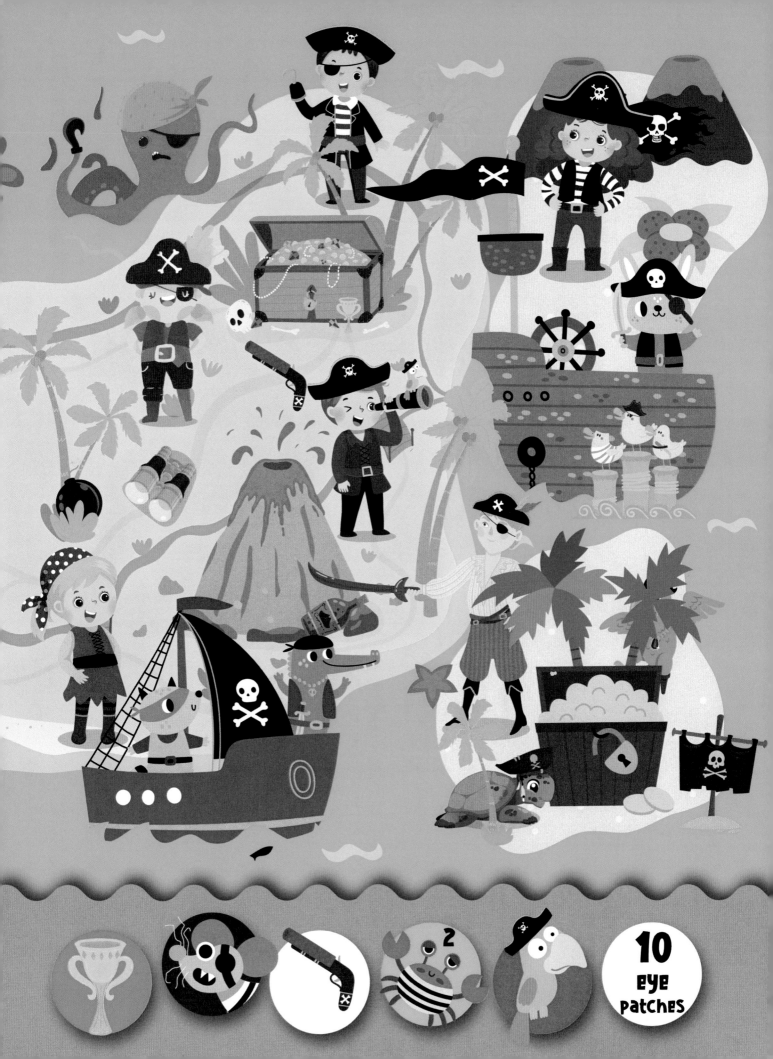

10 eye patches

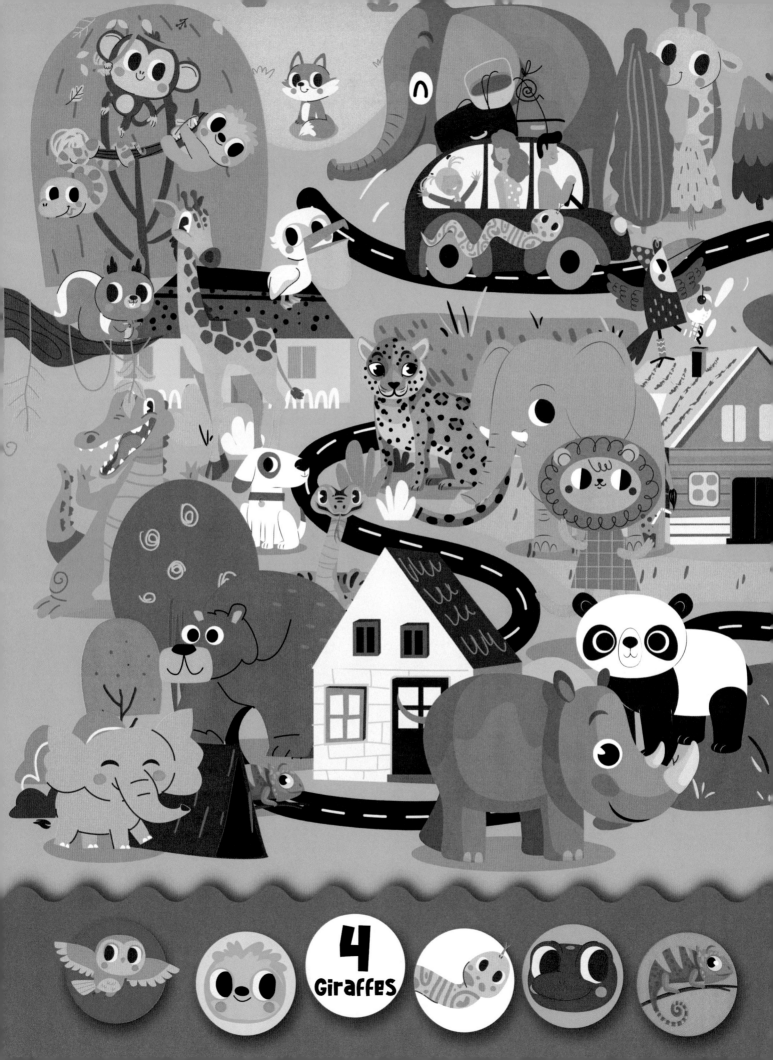

4
Giraffes

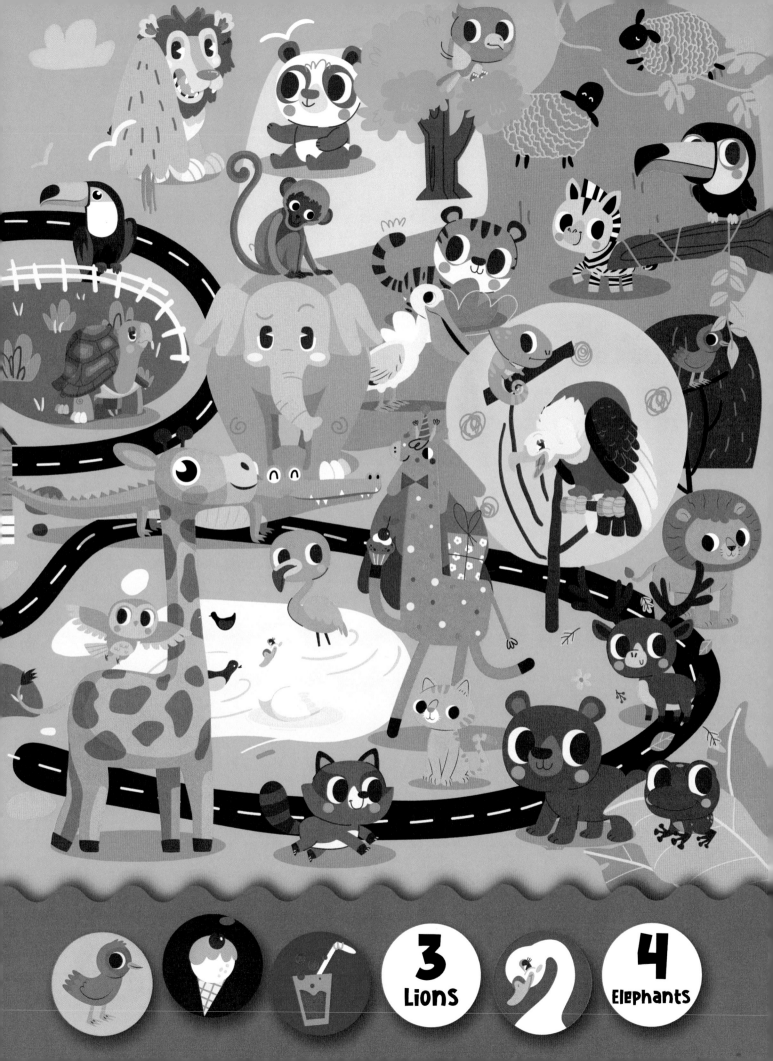

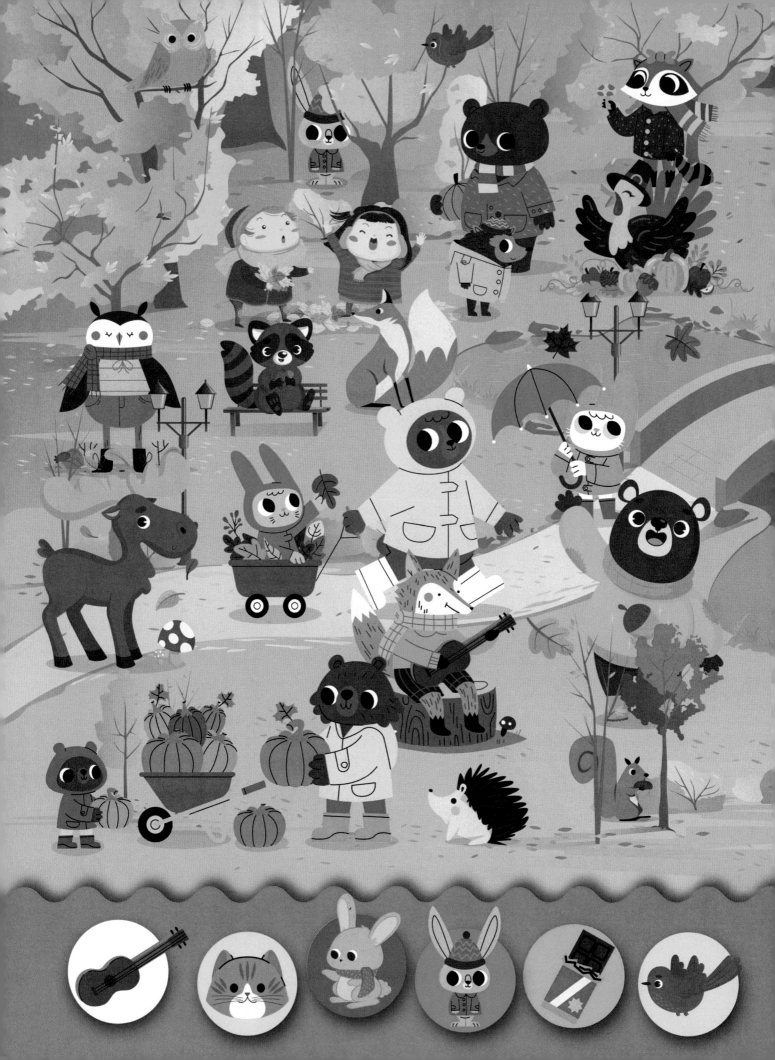

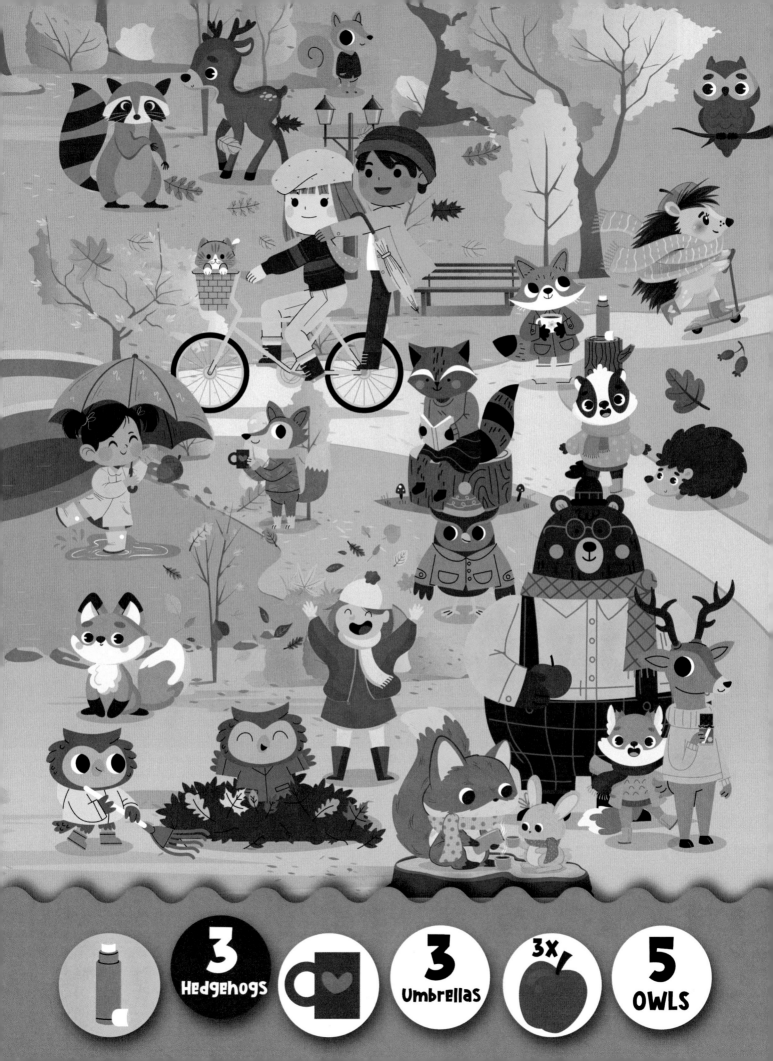

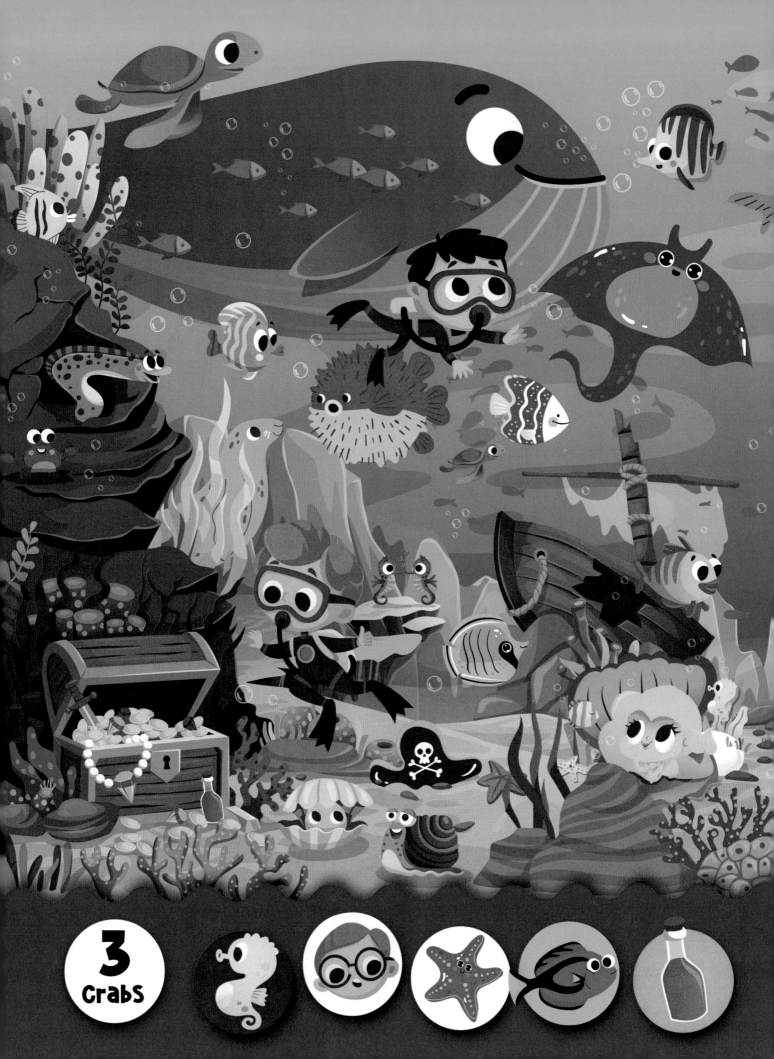

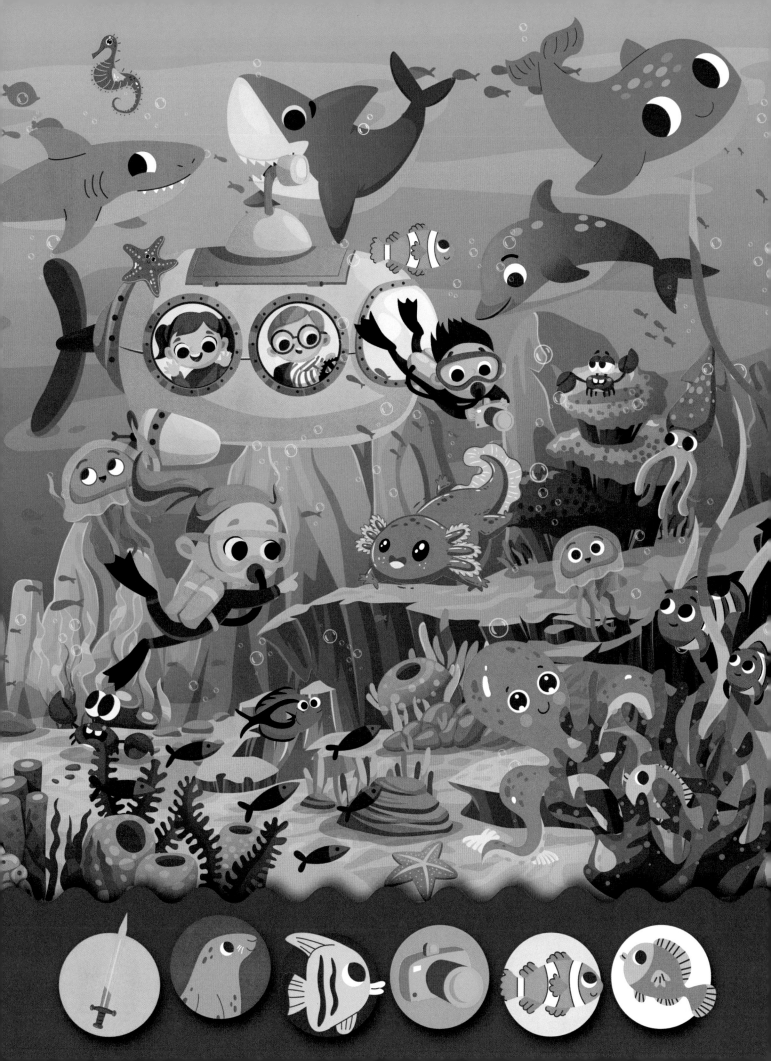

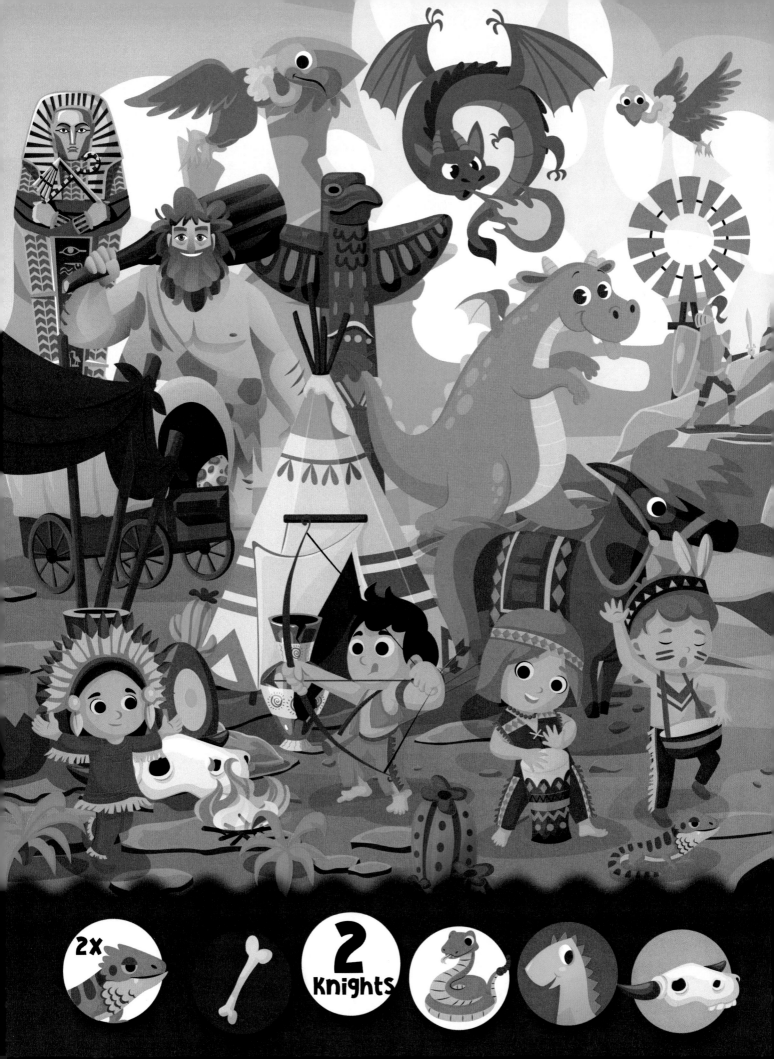

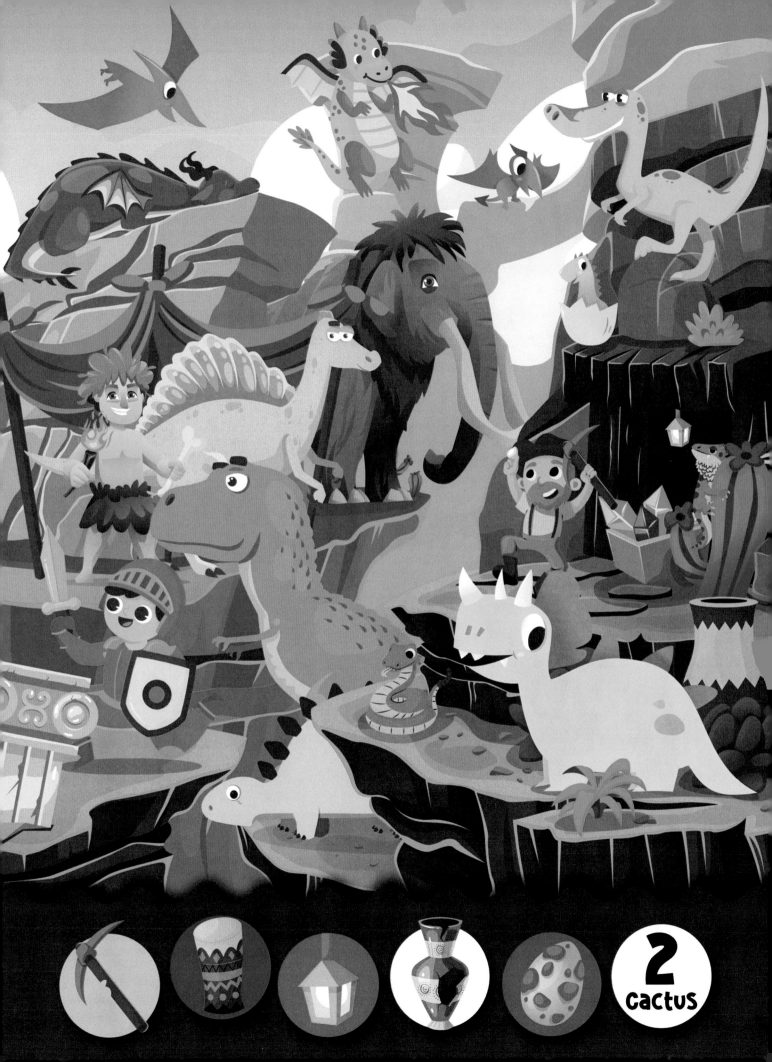

2 cactus

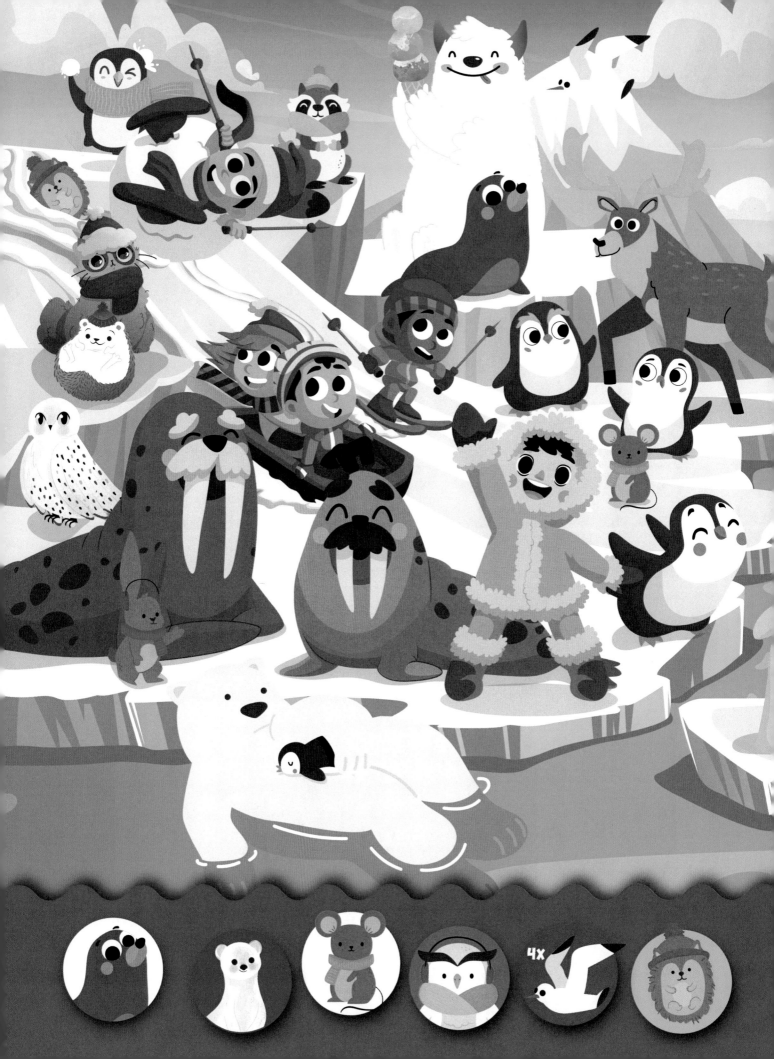

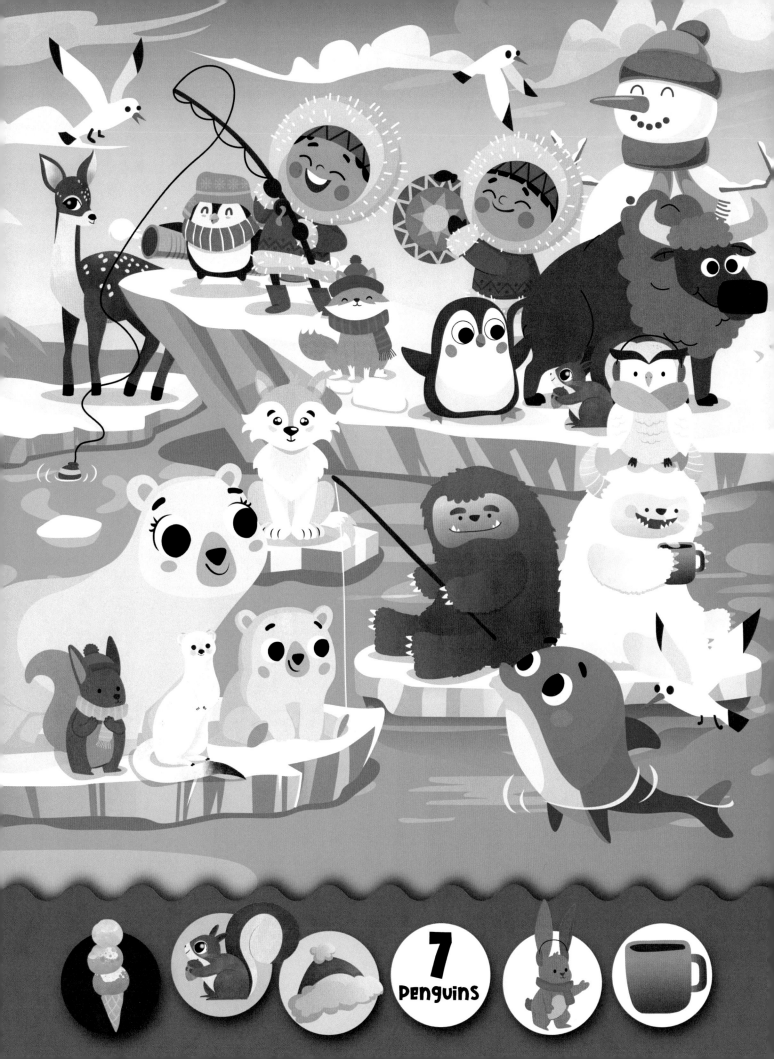

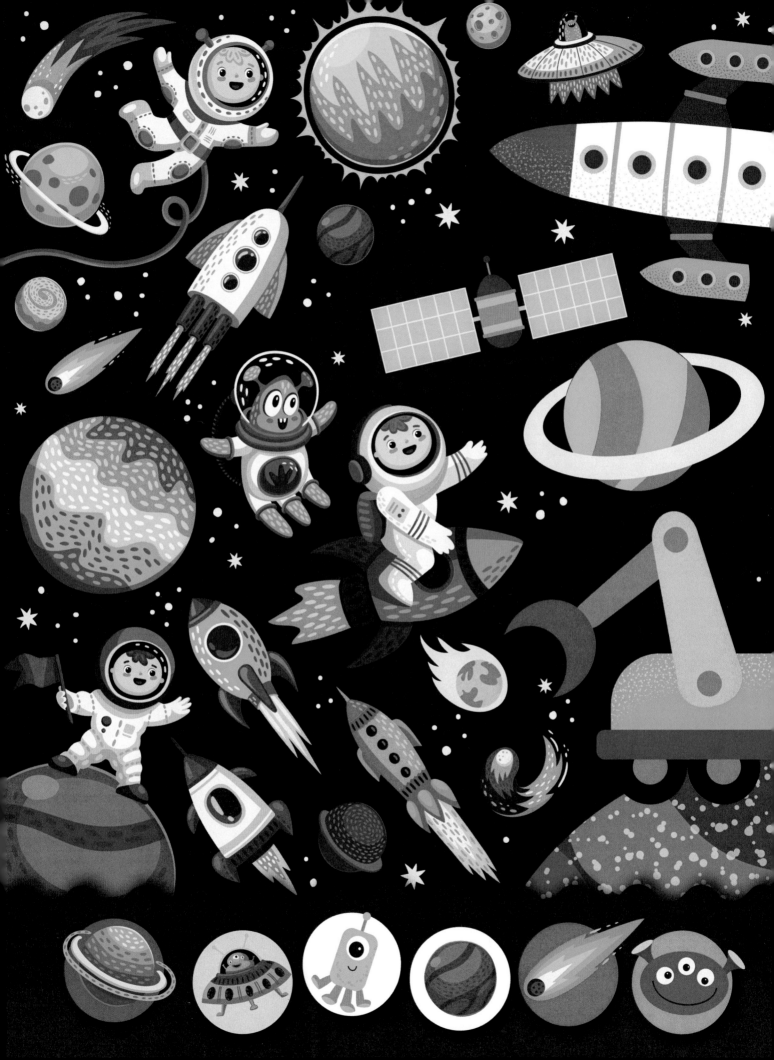

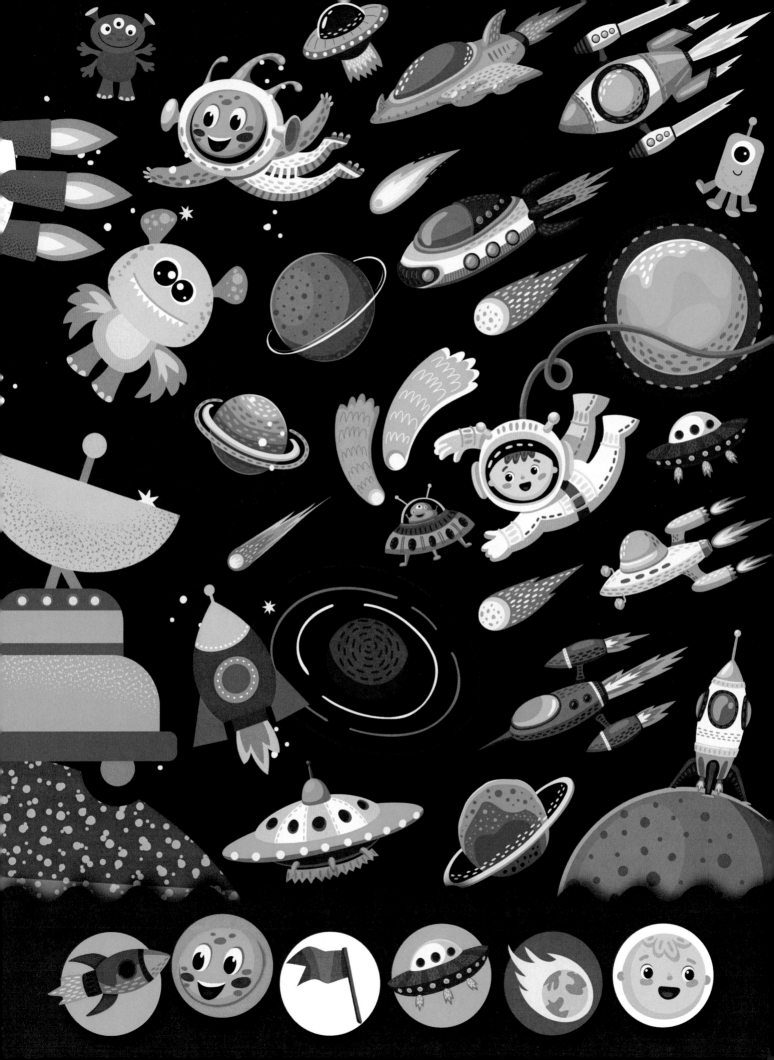

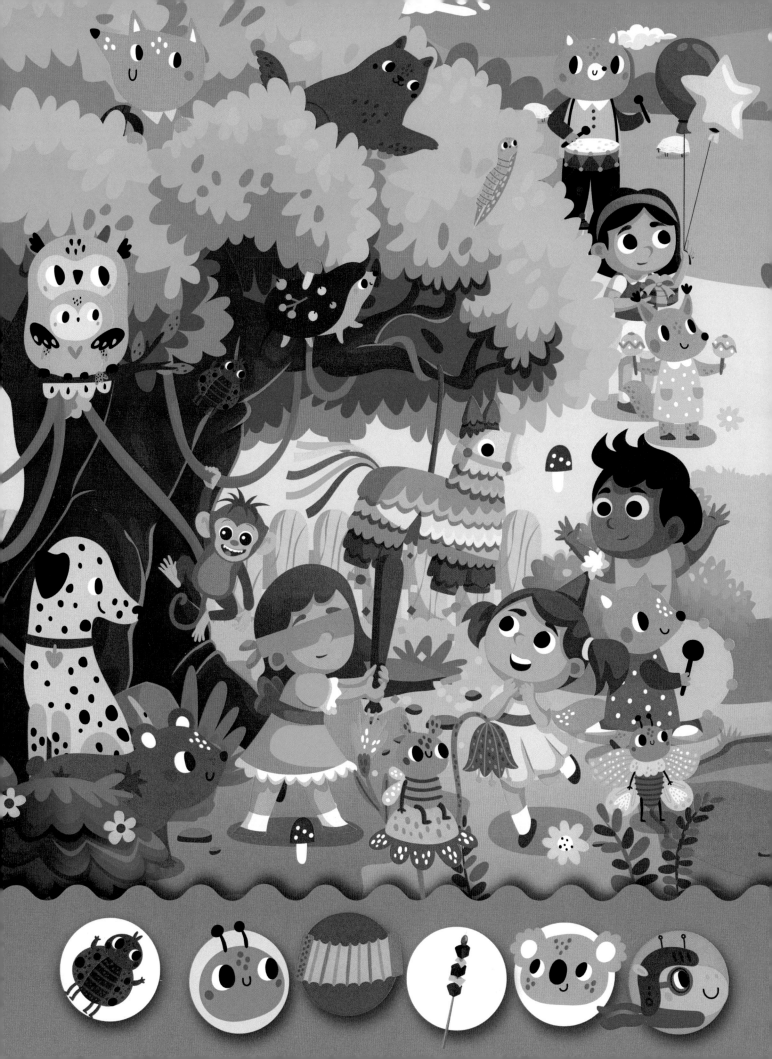

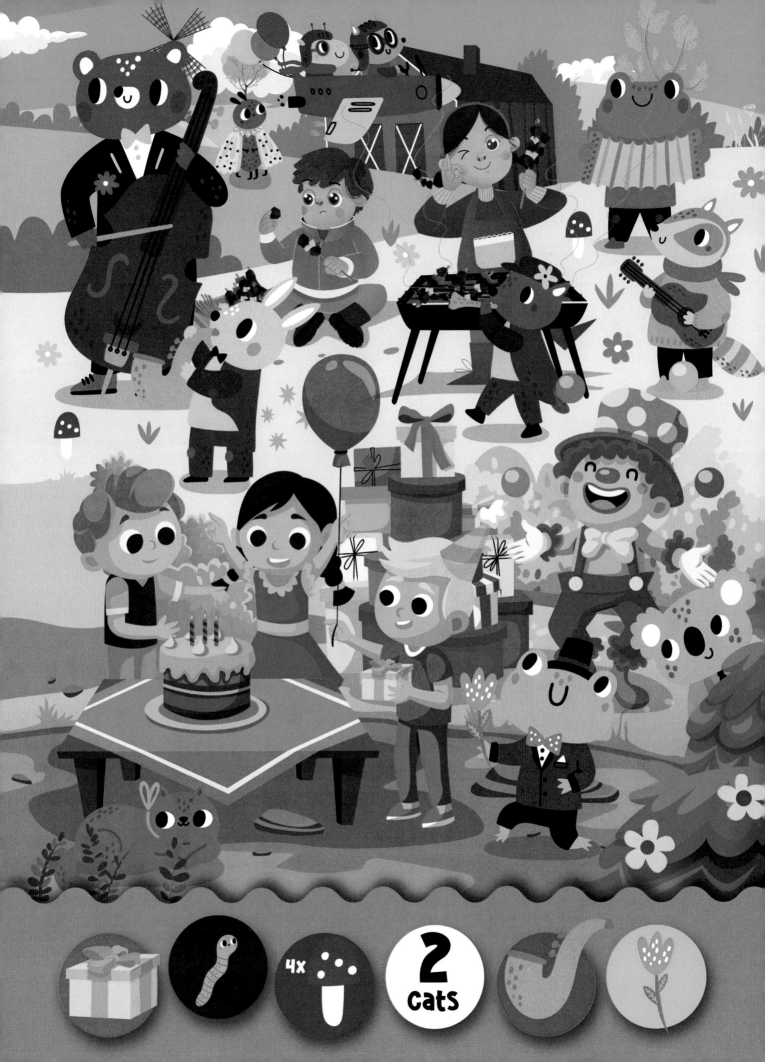

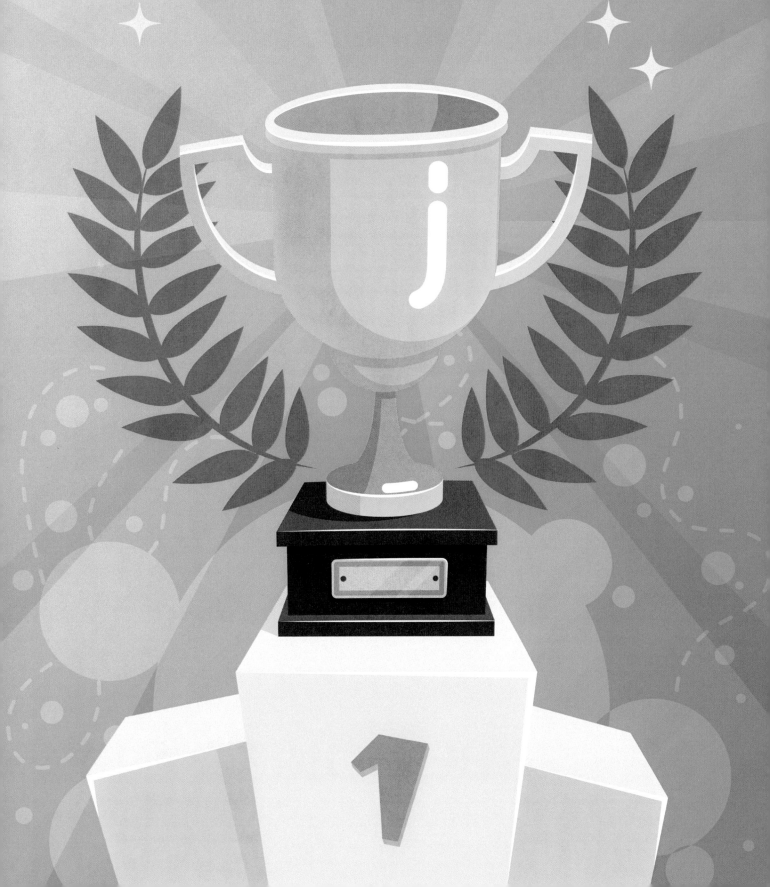

ACTIVITY GATO ©

36495645R00021